KU-169-130

SCIENCE FILES

HEAT & ENERGY

Steve Parker

Heinemann
LIBRARY

CONTENTS

6 SCIENCE OF HEAT

8 HEAT IS ENERGY

10 THE BIGGEST HEATER

12 SOURCES OF HEAT

14 HEAT AND TEMPERATURE

16 HEAT AND STATE

18 BIGGER, SMALLER

20 HOW HEAT TRAVELS

22 CONDUCTORS AND INSULATORS

24 WARMTH AND WEATHER

26 BODY HEAT

28 TOO HOT

30 FACTS & MEASUREMENTS

31 GLOSSARY

32 INDEX

WARNING!
All projects should be supervised by a responsible adult. Some need extra care and expert help, and are marked with a red box. Make sure the instructions are followed. *Never take risks.*

DUDLEY SCHOOLS LIBRARY
AND INFORMATION SERVICE

SCIENCE FILES

HEAT & ENERGY

Schools Library and Information Services

S00000670657

SCIENCE FILES – HEAT AND ENERGY
was produced by

David West 👫 **Children's Books**

7 Princeton Court
55 Felsham Road
London SW15 1AZ

Designer: Rob Shone
Editor: Gail Bushnell
Picture Research: Carlotta Cooper

First published in Great Britain by Heinemann
Library, Halley Court, Jordan Hill, Oxford
OX2 8EJ, part of Harcourt Education.
Heinemann is a registered trademark
of Harcourt Education Ltd.

Copyright © 2004 David West Children's Books

All rights reserved. No part of this publication may
be reproduced, stored in a retrieval system, or
transmitted in any form or by any means, electronic,
mechanical, photocopying, recording, or otherwise
without either prior written permission of the
Publishers or a licence permitting restricted copying in
the United Kingdom issued by the Copyright
Licensing Agency Ltd, 90 Tottenham Court Road,
London W1P 0LP.

08 07 06 05
10 9 8 7 6 5 4 3 2 1

ISBN 0 431 14315 3 (HB)
ISBN 0 431 14322 6 (PB)

L   **47960**

670657   SCH

JS36

British Library Cataloguing in Publication Data

Parker, Steve
Heat & energy. - (Science files)
1. Heat - Juvenile literature 2. Force and energy -
Juvenile literature 3. Heat - Experiments - Juvenile
literature 4. Force and energy - Experiments -
Juvenile literature
I. Title
536

Printed and bound in China

PHOTO CREDITS :
Abbreviations: t-top, m-middle, b-bottom, r-right,
l-left, c-centre.

Front cover - tl & r, bl & m - Corbis Images.
Pages 3 & 10–11, 4–5 & 18r, 6 both, 8t, 8–9, 10,
12l, 13t, 15r, 16, 16–17 both, 21, 24, 26t, 27t &
m - Corbis Images. 7l, 20 - DPMU0399 Images @
1999 Photodisc, Inc. 7tr - Daewoo Electronics
Sales UK. 11b - Solar & Heliospheric Observatory
/www.soho.nascom.nasa.gov. 19 - NASA. 24–25,
25t - Stock Images. 25m - National Oceanic &
Atmospheric Administration (NOAA). 28 - Rex
Features Ltd.

Every effort has been made to contact copyright
holders of any material reproduced in this book.
Any omissions will be rectified in subsequent
printings if notice is given to the publishers.

With special thanks to the models: Felix Blom,
Tucker Bryant and Margaux Monfared.

*An explanation of difficult words can be
found in the glossary on page 31.*

INTRODUCTION

Phew, this summer has been scorching! But it's better than wintertime, which can be freezing. We have to turn on the radiators and make warm drinks. Heat is so important in daily life. It keeps us and our surroundings comfortable, cooks our foods, is vital in industry and, with moisture, it encourages wildlife to thrive.

How it WORKS

These panels explain the science behind the projects, and the processes and principles that we see every day, but which we may not always understand!

PROJECTS

The projects are simple to do with supervision, using household items. Remember – scientists are cautious. They prepare equipment thoroughly, they know what should happen, and they *always* put safety first.

Heat is found across the Universe (left). Stars are gigantic burning balls of the substance hydrogen. They throw out unimaginable amounts of heat, as well as light and other kinds of energy.

Heat is not a special substance or material. It is the way substances move. More exactly, it is the movement of atoms.

THE ATOMIC WORLD

All substances, materials and matter are made of tiny particles called atoms, too small to see even under a powerful microscope. Atoms are hardly ever still. Each one tends to move or vibrate around a central point. The more atoms do this, the hotter they are.

Many factory processes rely on heat, especially for melting – turning a solid into a liquid. In a steelworks, the metal iron is heated until liquid and runny.

Heat and light often occur together because they can travel as the same basic form of energy (page 20).

Lack of heat is called cold. It slows many natural changes such as the rotting of food, which is why we use refrigerators.

THERMAL ENERGY

Heat is a form of atomic movement, and movement is a type of energy known as kinetic energy. The more atoms vibrate and move, the greater their heat content, which is called thermal energy. The science of heat, how it is made, how it moves and spreads, and how it changes into other forms of energy, is known as thermodynamics.

How it WORKS

In a solid, the atoms are arranged in a fixed pattern. With heat they move farther and faster, until they break out of the pattern and move freely. This is when the solid melts.

Cold atoms

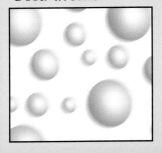

Hot atoms

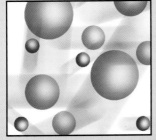

SOAKING UP HEAT

Different substances take up heat at different rates, known as specific heat capacity. Warm a ball-bearing and glass marble of equal size for equal times and place on butter. The one which has taken up most heat melts the most butter.

Ball bearing

Marble

Butter

Water trickling underground is boiled by great heat deep in the Earth's rocks. The hot water and steam spurt out as a geyser.

Energy causes change and makes things happen. When heat is present, this often causes change – depending on what is hot.

HEAT AND HAPPENINGS

We cannot see heat directly. A flame has heat, but what we see is its light energy. However we can see events which happen due to heat. These events may be changes in the form of a substance, like ice melting to water. They may be movements, such as the motion of a steam locomotive or jet engine. Or they may be the destructive change known as burning or combustion.

Burning is a chemical change or reaction between a substance (here natural gas) and oxygen in air.

A rocket burns fuel with oxygen to create white-hot gases. Space lacks oxygen so the rocket takes its own in chemical form.

CHANGING FORMS

Another feature of energy is that it can be altered or converted from one form to another. So heat can be made from other energy forms, like movement, electricity and chemicals, and also converted into them.

NO LOSS OR GAIN

Energy can be converted, but it is never lost or gained. The total amount of energy is conserved – it remains the same. The principle of energy conservation is extremely important in all areas of science.

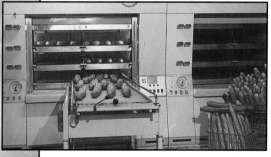

In baking, some heat is stored in chemical form in bread. The rest conducts through the oven walls to the surroundings.

How it **WORKS**

The metal is hotter than the water, so heat moves to raise the water temperature. Ice is colder, so heat moves from the water to melt it, lowering the water temperature. In both cases heat moves, but the total amount of heat energy stays the same.

Heat flows out from hot metal

Heat flows into cold ice

MOVING BUT CONSERVED

Thermometer

Heated metal

Ice cubes

Heat naturally spreads from hot objects to cold ones. Put a warm metal object and ice-cubes in separate glasses of cool water. Take the water temperature each minute.

THE BIGGEST HEATER

The Sun's surface has a temperature of 6000°C. It 'boils' continuously with incredible heat coming from the core, throwing out giant swirls of flames.

Deep below Earth's surface, rocks are so hot, they are melted and runny. We see them when a volcano erupts. However this heat is tiny compared to the heat from our nearest star – the Sun.

FUSION POWER

The temperature at the Earth's centre is 5500°C – but at the core of the Sun it is 15 million°C! The Sun glows almost white-hot by changing the very light substance hydrogen into slightly heavier helium. As this happens, hydrogen atoms join or fuse and tiny parts of them are destroyed, releasing heat, light and other energy.

Although people enjoy sunbathing, the Sun's ultra-violet rays can be harmful and cause skin cancer.

WARMTH FOR LIFE

In one second the Sun gives out heat energy equivalent to 90 billion nuclear explosions. The solar heat reaching Earth warms our planet to an average yearly temperature of 15°C, with some regions up to 50°C. Without the Sun, our temperature would plunge to −270°C and all life would cease.

A solar furnace receives the Sun's heat reflected from hundreds of mirrors and can reach 10,000°C.

SOLAR OVEN

Foil

Cling film

Cardboard box

Make a Sun-powered 'cooker' from a pizza-type carton, pie dish, cooking foil, cling film and a sample, such as butter, to heat.

WARNING Ensure a qualified adult helps with this project. Always be careful handling the pie dish, because it can become very hot in strong sunlight. Use oven gloves for protection.

How it **WORKS**

The Sun's heat and light shine straight into the cooking area and also reflect into it from the shiny lid. As the heat builds up, the cling film keeps it in the box, just as glass retains warmth in a greenhouse.

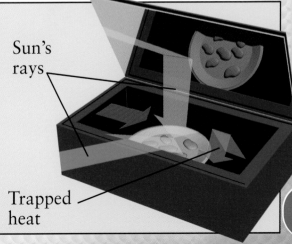

Sun's rays

Trapped heat

Satellites travelling near to the Sun have special heat-proof covers.

Ovens, central heating, light bulbs, car engines, candles – sources of heat are all around.

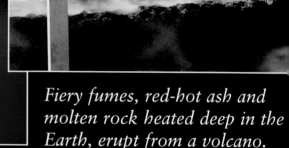

Natural gas fuel contains many kinds of hydrocarbons that burn well in air.

Fiery fumes, red-hot ash and molten rock heated deep in the Earth, erupt from a volcano.

NATURAL HEAT

Some sources of energy are converted or changed into heat by natural processes. The inside of the Earth is still very hot from its formation long ago and the crushing forces deep in the rocks. This geothermal (earth-heat) energy melts rock into the red-hot, liquid lava that bursts from volcanoes, and turns underground water into scalding steam.

How it WORKS

Fuels like petrol, diesel and natural gas contain linked hydrogen and carbon atoms, called hydrocarbons. Burning reacts these with the oxygen in air to break the bonds, form carbon dioxide gas and water, and release energy as heat and light.

MOVING HEAT

Any moving object has kinetic energy, and this can be changed into heat. As machine parts wear, rub and scrape together, they get hot. Lubricating oil not only lets them move smoothly, it also carries away some of the heat.

Rubbing or friction changes kinetic (moving) energy into heat, like these hot sparks from a grinding machine.

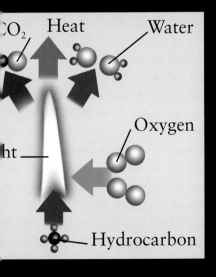

Decay makes heat, as in compost heaps, and when manure rots into fertilizer.

CO₂ — Heat — Water

Oxygen

ht

Hydrocarbon

HIGH-ENERGY FUELS

Fuels like petrol and coal contain lots of energy in the links or bonds which hold their atoms together. As the fuel burns, the atoms separate and the chemical bond energy changes into heat. In a nuclear reactor, the centres or nuclei of atoms split apart, releasing heat and radioactive energy.

Vast quantities of heat are generated in the reactor of a nuclear power station. The used fuel is very hot and stored in large cooling ponds.

13

Heat is a form of energy. Temperature is a measure of the level or degree of this energy. However, temperature is more complex than it seems.

TOTAL AMOUNT

The depth of a pond alone does not show the total amount of water it contains. Similarly, the temperature of an object alone does not measure the total amount of heat energy it contains. Extra information is needed, such as the weight or mass of the object.

RELATIVE AMOUNTS

Despite its limits, temperature is a useful measure in everyday life. It compares relative levels of heat in various objects and substances, and shows degrees of heat loss and gain. We measure a huge variety of temperatures – when cooking, in machines and industrial processes, in conditions for plants and animals, for weather, even in our bodies.

Chill-cabinets keep food fresher. Their temperature is taken often. If it rises, food may 'go bad' and decay, causing illness.

Some thermometers contain a liquid that enlarges or expands with heat, along the scale.

THERMOMETER

A thermometer can be made from dyed water, a cork with a hole, a straw, and two plastic bottles. A ring of card holds the small bottle inside the larger one. Make a card scale to show the water level.

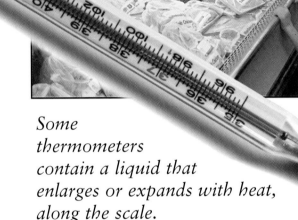

Plastic bottles

Card support

Cork

Straw

Card scale

Dyed water

A thermometer that switches a heating system on and off is called a thermostat. It keeps temperature constant, as in this glasshouse.

TEMPERATURE SCALES

Temperatures are measured by devices called thermometers. In daily life we use degrees Celsius, °C, but scientists use the Kelvin scale, K. A rise of 1 K is the same as 1°C, but the Kelvin scale starts at the lowest temperature possible, absolute zero. 0 K is the same as −273.15°C.

How it **WORKS**

Put the thermometer out in the sunshine and watch the water level descend on the scale! The Sun's heat warms the air in the upper bottle. This gets bigger or expands (page 18) into the straw, pushing the water level down. Try putting the thermometer in the fridge!

The planet Mercury is so near the Sun, its 'day' temperature is 450°C. 'Night' on the other, dark side is −170°C!

HEAT AND STATE

A ship floats on the very common substance we call water. However it may be sunk by water too – if that water is frozen into an iceberg.

THREE STATES

Water is a liquid. It can flow and change shape. Liquid is one of three forms of a substance, called states. The other two states are solid, like iron and glass, and gas, such as oxygen and nitrogen in air.

DEPENDING ON HEAT

The state of a substance depends on how much heat it contains, as indicated by its temperature. Water is liquid at everyday temperatures, but if its heat is taken away, its state changes. It turns into hard ice, called solidifying. If ice receives heat it changes back into liquid water, known as melting.

Water is the most common everyday substance that exists in all three states – here as a liquid.

Water heated to more than 100°C deep underground emerges as a gas mixed with tiny droplets – steam.

If enough heat is taken away to reduce water's temperature below 0°C, it freezes into ice, like these icicles.

GIVE AND TAKE AWAY

More heat makes water change state again into gas, water vapour. This happens when water boils into steam. Almost all substances can exist as solid, liquid or gas, but mostly at extreme temperatures. Rocks do not melt until 1000°C.

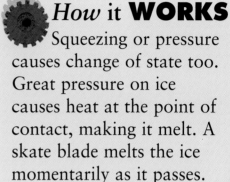

In the cold ice-hockey arena, the players' speed depends on tiny patches of heat (right).

How it WORKS

Squeezing or pressure causes change of state too. Great pressure on ice causes heat at the point of contact, making it melt. A skate blade melts the ice momentarily as it passes. So ice-skaters should really be called water-skaters.

Downward pressure of skater melts ice

Metal blade
Thin water layer
Ice

SLICE THE ICE

Here's how to slice ice in two as if cutting butter. Wedge an ice cube into a bottle neck. Join two weights by a piece of thin wire. Drape the wire over the ice cube, and wait. Slowly the wire cuts down through the ice. In the freezer, the 'cut' may 'heal' itself!

Ice cube

Bottle

Wire

Weight

18 BIGGER, SMALLER

Air expands with heat too. The hot air in a balloon is lighter, for its volume, than the air around and so it rises.

Thermometers, heating controls, car engine cooling systems, buckled railway lines in summer – these all happen when objects are heated and get bigger.

CHANGE IN HEAT = CHANGE IN SIZE

Heat makes the tiny atoms of an object or substance move, or vibrate, more. As this happens they also become slightly farther apart, making the whole object bigger. This effect is called expansion. As heat is taken away from an object and it becomes colder the reverse happens. It gets slightly smaller, known as contraction.

A barrel's metal hoops are heated before being put over the wooden slats. The hoops cool, contract and squeeze the slats tight.

EXPANSION RATES

The rate of expansion varies between different substances. In general, metals expand faster than non-metals. Some metals, however, expand faster than others and are used in thermostats.

FIT TO BUST

Expansion is usually tiny, but it can cause trouble. Railway lines expand in hot weather, so they need spaces between them to prevent buckling. Planes that fly at supersonic speeds get very hot and will expand many centimetres.

How it WORKS

A thermostat contains a strip of two different metals. As it warms, one metal expands faster. This bends the strip and breaks the electrical contact to turn off the heating.

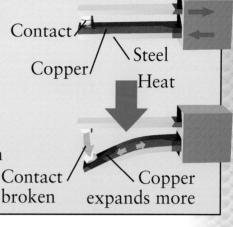

Contact
Copper
Steel
Heat
Contact broken
Copper expands more

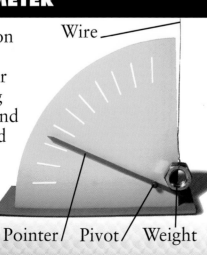

Although the 'Blackbird' plane was made of titanium metal, which expands little with heat, it still had tiny expansion gaps. These meant that at supersonic speeds, when it got very hot, the parts fitted together perfectly.

EXPANSION METER

By using an expansion meter you can see a wire becoming longer with heat. A hanging weight rests on the end of the pointer, behind the pivot. Heat the wire with a hairdryer and watch the pointer rise up the scale.

Wire

Pointer / Pivot / Weight

How it WORKS

The wire warms and lengthens. This lowers the weight on the pointer's short end, so its longer end pivots up the scale. Repeat the test for copper wire, steel wire, cotton thread and plastic line.

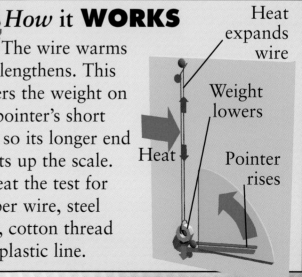

Heat expands wire
Weight lowers
Heat
Pointer rises

How it WORKS
A warm drink loses heat in all three ways. The heat energy conducts into the spoon and to a lesser extent the mug. It is convected away by moving air. And it radiates from all the warm surfaces as infrared or 'heat' rays.

The flames of a fire lose much of their heat as radiation, as 'heat' or infrared rays which spread outwards from them.

You can feel the warm air from a fire, and see the glow, but don't touch or you'll be burned!

WAYS TO TRAVEL

Heat moves from place to place in three ways. Firstly, conduction is when two objects are in contact or touching and heat seeps or flows between them. The second way, convection, is when a gas such as air takes up heat from a hot object and moves or flows, carrying the heat energy with it. Liquids such as water flow and carry heat by convection.

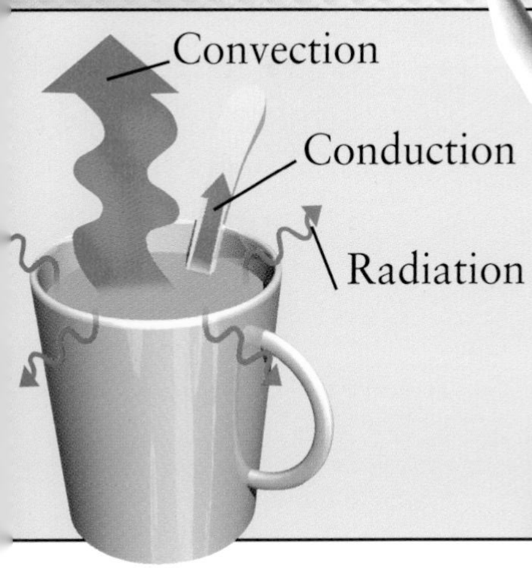

Convection

Conduction

Radiation

The walls of a furnace get very hot as conduction allows heat to seep through them from the interior.

Sun-warmed air expands and flows upwards. Gliders use these convection currents to lift them higher.

THE THIRD WAY

Heat also moves as rays or waves called infrared radiation. The rays are made of magnetic and electrical energy, similar to light rays. Often we see a mix of infrared and light as the glow of a hot object.

MOVING THROUGH NOTHING

Both conduction and convection need an object or substance for the heat to travel. Radiation does not. Infrared waves can travel through the nothingness of a vacuum. Which is just as well, because space is a vacuum, and the Sun's heat (and light) pass through it to Earth.

Gloves keep our hands warm in cool weather, and also keep our hands cool when we touch warm objects. How?

A car's exhaust system conducts away some of the engine's heat and 'glows' at very high temperature.

STOPPING HEAT

Heat flows through and between substances by conduction (see previous page). Some substances allow heat through very easily, and are conductors. Other substances, like the material of gloves, carry heat very badly. They are known as insulators.

A motorcycle engine has metal cooling fins (see inset). Their large surface area conducts the engine's heat away to the air.

BEAD RACE

Pour some hot water into a bowl. Put a plastic stick, metal knife and wooden spoon in the bowl. Stick a small bead to each with butter. Watch to see which bead slides down the fastest.

Warm air rises, so much heat is lost through a house roof. Fibre-type insulation cuts the loss.

The space shuttle has high-performance insulating tiles on its underside.

How it WORKS

The best conductor carries heat the fastest to melt the butter and release the bead. Materials that do not conduct heat are good insulators. A thermos flask's stopper stops heat conduction. The vacuum also prevents conduction, as well as convection. The silvered sides prevent radiation.

Stopper

Vacuum

Silvered glass

SLOWER

Most metals are good heat or thermal conductors. Wood, plastic, glass, ceramic and fabric are thermal insulators. These materials are used to control heat's flow and movement in cars, cookers, clothes, houses and even space rockets.

INTENSE HEAT

A spacecraft returning to Earth re-enters the atmosphere at great speed. Friction with the air creates intense heat, over 1600°C. Special insulation on the craft stops it burning up.

23

The Sun's heat provides far more than warm summer days. It produces winds, clouds and the rest of weather.

PATCHY HEAT

Some areas of the Earth's surface, like dark rocks, soak up more heat than others. This difference causes patchy heating of the air too. Warm air rises, cool air moves along to take its place, and the result is wind.

BLOWING ALONG

The Sun's warmth also turns water in lakes, rivers and oceans into vapour in the air. This powers the water cycle. And as winds blow, they cause ripples on water. At sea the ripples build into huge waves that crash on the shore and wear away the land. So solar heat even shapes our coastlines.

Clouds swirl in winds across our world – all due to the energy of the Sun's heat.

Billions of tiny water droplets in clouds are raised by solar heat and fall due to gravity.

WATER CYCLE

How it **WORKS**
Solar heat energy evaporates water – changes it to invisible water vapour, which is warm and rises into the air. This moist air blows up mountains where conditions are colder. The cooled moisture condenses, or turns back into water, as droplets that form clouds, mist, rain, sleet and snow.

In a drought the Sun's warmth evaporates a lake's water and then cracks the mud with its heat.

LIFE'S NEEDS

Life thrives best in warm, damp places like tropical rainforests. The Sun's heat brings the warmth directly, and the moisture indirectly, by the water cycle. Without them, living things perish.

Lack of heat means water falls as frozen flakes of snow. Blizzards, gales and extreme weather affect daily life.

Sun

4 Cooled vapour forms clouds and rain

5 Rain fills rivers

3 Moist air rises and cools

2 Moist air moves inland

1 Sun's heat evaporates water in seas, lakes and rivers

6 Rivers flow to sea

Make a simple 'water cycle' with a plastic sheet, bowl and tumbler. Leave in a warm place. Heat evaporates the water, which condenses on the plastic's underside and runs down to the tumbler.

Plastic with weight in centre to form a cone shape

Tumbler

Water in bowl

25

BODY HEAT

Some animals make their own heat to stay warm. Others are at the mercy of their surroundings.

Many mammals cannot sweat effectively because of their fur, so they pant away the heat instead.

SLOW-BURNING BODIES

Birds and mammals are 'warm-blooded'. Some of the energy contained in their food, in chemical form, is changed by a 'slow-burn' process in the body to release heat gradually. So birds and mammals can stay warm and active even in cold places like polar regions and high on mountains. However, they also have ways of keeping cool in hot weather.

Great activity in hot conditions brings a risk of overheating. Splashes of water aid sweat to help cool the body.

EVAPORATION

Our body temperature should be 37°C. A rise, hyperthermia, can be very harmful. The body reacts by sweating. Tiny beads of sweat ooze on to the skin. See how sweat works with two thermometers. Wrap the bulb of one with wet cotton-wool. Blow them both with a hair-dryer set on 'cool'. Which cools fastest?

In frozen Antarctica penguins have both thick feathers and blubber to keep in body heat.

Reptiles like the iguana lizard become less active as conditions get cooler.

STAYING WARM

To prevent heat loss from their bodies, 'warm-blooded' animals have insulation. Birds have feathers and mammals have fur. In the water a furry covering would be soggy and ineffective. So full-time water mammals like whales have a thick layer of insulating fat, blubber, under the skin.

COLD-BLOODED

Nearly all other animals, like snakes, fish and insects, are 'cold-blooded'. Their bodies remain much the same in temperature as their surroundings. In cold weather they hardly move and hide away for safety.

Read temperature on scale

Uncovered bulb

Wet cotton-wool around bulb

How it WORKS

Water needs warmth to evaporate into vapour. As air blows the thermometers, the water in the cotton-wool draws heat from its bulb to evaporate. So the reading on this thermometer is lower than on the other one. Sweat cools the body in the same way.

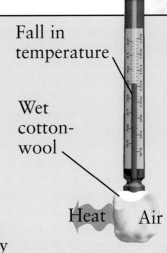

Fall in temperature

Wet cotton-wool

Heat   Air

Fires rage when wind brings continuing supplies of fresh oxygen-rich air to fan the flames.

Objects with a temperature above about 50°C feel hot. This warns us to keep clear, since heat burns our bodies and smoke harms our airways and lungs. Fires kill – so beware!

STARVED OF OXYGEN

Flames, like animals, must have oxygen to survive. This gas makes up one-fifth of air. It takes part in the chemical reactions of combustion or burning (see page 8). Prevent oxygen reaching a fire, using foam, a blanket or a heavy gas like carbon dioxide, and the flames 'suffocate'.

HELP!

Some fire-extinguishers use these various methods of preventing oxygen reaching a fire. Fires can also be put out by removing the heat from the flames, by using water. They will also go out if they have no more fuel left to burn.

Spraying foam on to a fire prevents oxygen in the air from reaching it, so the flames soon go out.

In remote places, such as forests, planes and helicopters are used to drop water or fire-retardant chemicals directly on to wildfires.

SNUFFED OUT

Put a small night-light candle on a support in a bowl of water. Carefully place a heat-proof glass over it. Gradually the flame shrinks and goes out.

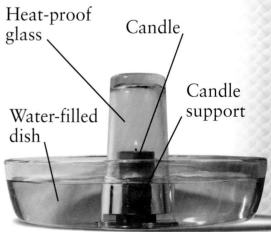

Heat-proof glass

Candle

Water-filled dish

Candle support

WARNING Ensure a qualified adult helps with this project. Always be careful when lighting the candle and placing the glass over it. Allow the glass to cool before removing it.

How it WORKS

The covered candle can only burn using oxygen in the glass. Once consumed, the flame dies. Also water is pushed up into the glass to replace the lost oxygen.

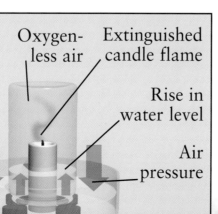

Oxygen-less air

Extinguished candle flame

Rise in water level

Air pressure

TEMPERATURE SCALES – °C AND °F

The everyday temperature scale is degrees Celsius, °C. This is based on two set points, the melting point of ice to water and the boiling point of water to steam. The temperature difference between them is divided into 100 units, from 0°C to 100°C. Centigrade is now rarely used as an equivalent. The Fahrenheit scale is still used in some regions. Its set points are 32°F for ice melting and 212°F for water boiling.
• To change °F to °C – take away 32 from °F, multiply by 5, divide by 9.
• To change °C to °F – multiply °C by 9, divide by 5, add 32.

TEMPERATURE SCALE – K

The scientific scale of temperature is Kelvin (without the word 'degrees' or the symbol °). A temperature difference of 1°C is the same as the difference of 1 K. However the scales start at different places, with 0 K being absolute zero, as below.

ABSOLUTE ZERO

The coldest possible temperature anywhere in the Universe is absolute zero, when atoms and molecules stop moving altogether and so have no energy of motion or heat.
Absolute zero
• 0 K = –273.15°C = –459.67°F

JOULES AND CALORIES

Any kind of energy, including heat, can be measured in units known as joules. A standard one-kilowatt electric heater gives out up to 1000 joules per second. The human body produces around 80–130 joules per second while asleep or resting. (Heat and other forms of energy, such as chemical energy in foods, used to be measured in calories. One calorie equals 4.2 joules.)

MELTING AND BOILING POINTS

Here are some examples of melting points (MPs) and boiling points (BPs), all in °C:
• Oxygen   MP –218   BP –183
• Alcohol   MP –114   BP   78.3
• Mercury   MP –38.8   BP 356.6
• Cooking oil MP –20   BP 200+
• Water   MP   0   BP 100
• Aluminium MP 660   BP 2467
• Iron   MP 1535   BP 2750
• Titanium   MP 1660   BP 3287

Mercury is used in standard thermometers and alcohol in low-temperature ones, due to the temperature ranges when they expand.

TEMPERATURE RANGES (°C)

500 million	Scientific research into plasmas
15 million	Centre of the Sun
6000	Surface of the Sun
5500	Centre of the Earth
1000	Lava (molten rock)
220	High cooking temperature
100	Boiling point of water
58	Hottest weather (Libya)
50	Hot bath water
37	Human body
20–25	Room temperature
5	Typical fridge
0	Melting point of water
–30	Typical freezer
–78.5	'Dry ice' (solid carbon dioxide)
–89.2	Coldest weather (Antarctica)
–200	Liquid nitrogen (ultracold or cryogenic storage)
–273.15	Absolute zero

GLOSSARY

atom
The smallest particle of an element, made up of a central nucleus surrounded by electrons.

boil
To change a liquid to a gas, usually by adding heat.

combustion
The process of burning, in which a chemical substance combines with oxygen to produce heat (and usually light, too).

condense
To change from a gas to a liquid, usually by taking away heat.

conduction
When energy, such as heat or electricity, moves through an object or from one object to another.

convection
Movement of heat through a liquid or gas by currents, as when rising air carries heat with it.

evaporate
To change from a liquid to a vapour or gas.

geothermal
'Earth heat' or 'ground heat' – the vast quantities of heat deep inside the Earth.

melt
To change from a solid to a liquid, usually by adding heat. 'Molten' means 'melted'.

radiation
Energy sent out or given off, usually in the form of electro-magnetic waves, such as radio waves, infrared or heat, and light.

solar
To do with the Sun. Solar energy is a mixture of heat, light and other energy radiated by the Sun.

solidify
To change from a liquid to a solid, usually by taking away heat.

absolute zero 15, 30
animals 26–27
atoms 5, 10, 12, 18, 30, 31

'Blackbird' plane 19
boiling 17, 30, 31
burning 8, 12–13, 28, 31

carbon dioxide 12, 13, 28, 30
Celsius scale 15, 30
chemical energy 13
chemicals 8–9
combustion 8, 28, 31
condensation 24–25, 31
conduction 20–21, 22, 31
contraction 18–19
convection 20–21, 31

electricity 9
energy 5, 9–10, 20, 30
evaporation 24–25, 26, 31
expansion 14, 18–19

fire, dangers of 28–29
friction 13, 23
fuels 12–13

geothermal energy 12, 31

heat
    as energy 6–7, 8–9, 30
    capacity 7
    flow 9, 20–21
    sources 12–13
helium 10
hydrocarbons 12
hydrogen 10
hyperthermia 26

ice 9, 16, 17, 30
insulation 22–23, 27

Kelvin scale 15, 30
kinetic energy 6, 13

light 5, 6, 8, 10, 13, 31

melting 5, 16, 17, 30, 31

Mercury (planet) 15

nuclear energy 13

oxygen 8, 9, 28, 31

radiation 20–21, 31

solar energy 11, 24, 31
solidifying 16, 31
stars 5, 10
states of matter 16–17
Sun 10–11, 24, 30

temperature 11, 14–15, 16, 30
thermodynamics 7
thermometers 9, 14–15, 18, 27, 31
thermostat 15, 19

ultra-violet rays 10

vibrations 5, 18

water 16–17, 24–25 30
weather 24–25, 30